I0510512

- This **NOTEBOOK** belongs to -

Jocs press

www.ingramcontent.com/pod-product-compliance
Lightning Source LLC
Chambersburg PA
CBHW021417210526
45463CB00001B/417
9781694386571